Young Writers PRESENTS

MONSTER ACROSTICS

Poetic Charms

First published in Great Britain in 2025 by:
YoungWriters®
Est. 1991

Young Writers
Remus House
Coltsfoot Drive
Peterborough
PE2 9BF
Telephone: 01733 890066
Website: www.youngwriters.co.uk

All Rights Reserved
Book Design by Neila Cepulionyte
© Copyright Contributors 2025
Softback ISBN 978-1-83685-536-1
Printed and bound in the UK by BookPrintingUK
Website: www.bookprintinguk.com
YB0643T

Foreword

Welcome Reader,

For Young Writers' latest competition Monster Acrostics, we asked primary school pupils to create a monster then write an acrostic poem about it. The acrostic is a fantastic introduction to poetry writing as it comes with a built-in structure, allowing children to focus on their creativity and vocabulary choice.

We live and breathe creativity here at Young Writers and we want to pass our love of the written word onto the next generation – what better way to do that than to celebrate their writing by publishing it in a book!

Featuring all kinds of crazy creatures, strange beasts and mythical monsters, this anthology is brimming with imagination and creativity, showcasing the blossoming writing skills of these young poets. They have brought their creations to life using the power of words, resulting in some brilliant and fun acrostic poems!

Each awesome little poet in this book should be super proud of themselves! We hope you will delight in these poems as much as we have.

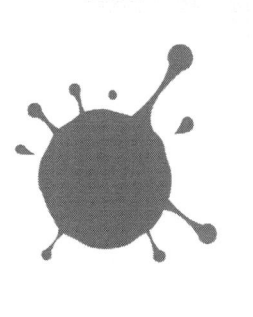

Contents

Goodrich CofE Primary School, Ross-On-Wye

Erin Williford (6)	1
Imogen Brewer (5)	2
Leilani Powell (7)	3
Benji Cowan (6)	4
Flora Wimperis (6)	5
Daisy Ryan (6)	6
Ayda Jones (6)	7
Cai Malbon (7)	8
Frankie Stretton (5)	9
Elsie Neal (6)	10
Aster Summers (7)	11
Isaac Boyd (7)	12
Ralph Radbone (7)	13
Gracie Hallett (7)	14
Asa James (6)	15
Albert Symonds (6)	16
William Brewer (6)	17
Eleanor Johnson (6)	18
Alys Townsend (5)	19
Merry Cox (6)	20
Gabriel Beattie (7)	21
Andie Emblen (6)	22
Sammy Van Marsh (6)	23
Athena Jones-Davies (5)	24
Freddy Byrne (7)	25

Hall Orchard CE Primary School, Barrow upon Soar

Jack Moore (7)	26
Charlie Padgett (5)	27
Evie Caren (5)	28
Isaac Kalsi (5)	29
Harlow Bowler (6)	30
Martha Graham-Hind (5)	31
Emilia S (6)	32
Miller Walton (6)	33
Oliver Nutting (6)	34
Harry Moulds (6)	35
Violet Laywood (6)	36
Sophia Penn (5)	37
Sophie Jasper (5)	38
Eloise Riley (7)	39
Huey Woodrup (7)	40
Arthur Goddard (6)	41
Forest Stewart (6)	42
Heidi Jewitt (6)	43
Abel Sharpe (6)	44
Frankie Ross (6)	45
Eden Turner (5)	46
Mia Seaton (5)	47
Morgan Hitchcock (5)	48
Elijah Nagra (5)	49
Daisy Vickers (5)	50
Owen Clithero (5)	51
Leo Hopkinson (5)	52
Teddy Barkby (6)	53
Arthur Evans (6)	54
Isobella Morris (7)	55
Anaiya Arefin (6)	56
Archie Savage (5)	57
Reuben Landon (5)	58
Emily Williams (6)	59
Louis Young (5)	60
Ellie Marston (5)	61
Hussein Abbas (6)	62
George Squires (6)	63
Lily Broderick (7)	64

George Hickling (6)	65
Halle Woodrup (5)	66
Francesca R (6)	67
Jack Perkins (5)	68
Adelaide Quinn (6)	69
Bethan Noble (5)	70
James Slade (6)	71
Piper Winfield (5)	72
Jackson Turner (6)	73
Maryam Abbas (5)	74
Freya Adams (5)	75
Maxwell Smith (5)	76
Theo Dunn (5)	77
Willow Pymm (5)	78
Max Copeman (5)	79
Cassandra Crawshaw (5)	80
William Morris (6)	81
Jago Cohill IV (6)	82
Lydia Andrews (6)	83
Neve Morris (5)	84
Ivy Hamilton (5)	85

Hurst Park Primary School, West Molesey

Perla Shehaj (6)	86
Isabelle Levitt (7)	87
Lily Clarke (6)	88
Jack N (7)	89
Miri (6)	90
Ruby Pemberton (6)	91
Emily Jacklin (7)	92
Akira De Rijk (6)	93
Alba Wragg (6)	94
Adam Nowogrodzki (7)	95
Ryan Rouine (6)	96
Chloe Chapman (6)	97

Mossvale Primary School, Paisley

Stephanie McGonigle (7)	98
Raaeid Jumahi Ahmed (7)	99
Harper Logan (7)	100
Callen Fairbairn	101

Beth Beaton (7)	102

Muirhouse Primary School, Motherwell

Molly Colquhoun (6)	103
Alex Neary (6)	104
Latifa Abasi (6)	105
Reggie Buchan (6)	106
Reegan Macdonald (6)	107
Ariannah O'Connor (6)	108
Logan Rattray (7)	109
Skyla McLean (8)	110
Holly Montgomery (7)	111
Oliver Steele (7)	112
Amelia McCulloch (6)	113
Louie Stewart (7)	114
Bella Richardson (6)	115
Ezra Baxter (7)	116

Park Lane Primary School, Wembley

Arjun Singh Rathore (7)	117
Allanah Trinidad (6)	118
Myra Patel (6)	119
Arhaan Momin (7)	120
Jacob Rai (6)	121
Amay Gupta (6)	122
Nitya Patel (7)	123
Priyansh Solanki (7)	124
Kiriana Bellingy (7)	125
Kyle Allen (7)	126
Miruzaini Ravichandran (7)	127
Ilyas Nouar (6)	128
Aiden D'Silva (7)	129
Ayaan Hanif (7)	130
Emma Taraba Donati (7)	131
Anha Jadav (8)	132
Nylah Jackson (7)	133
Mayra Patil (6)	134
Anna Bacso (7)	135

Romanby Primary School, Romanby

Eric Botwright (7)	136
George Hartley (7)	137
Layla Grant (7)	138
Archie Miles (7)	139
Joshua Morris (7)	140
Evie Parkes (7)	141
Matthew Paul (6)	142
Lukas Bishop (6)	143
Thomas Field (6)	144

St Dominic's Primary School, Airdrie

Lucilla Gargaro (8)	145
Cierra Lafferty (7)	146
Maya Szydlowska (7)	147
Willow Drummond (7)	148
Sara Marczak (7)	149
Anthony Adeoye (7)	150
Katie N McAspurren (8)	151
Reuben Graham (7)	152
Charlotte Watson (7)	153
Anton Hamill (7)	154

St George's School, Edgbaston

Aveline Gazzani (5)	155
Abaan Shams (5)	156
Ajai Choudhary (7)	157
Abigail Tonks (6)	158
Sabina Tomenchuk (6)	159
Amelia Boutefnouchet (5)	160
Zayan Nasar (6)	161
Danyil Mamus (6)	162
Arya Adil (5)	163

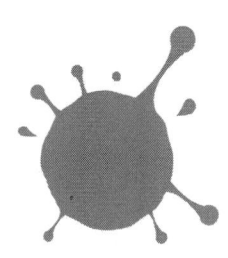

The Acrostics

Grumpy

G rowls a lot.
R umbly tummy.
U ndie scratcher.
M onkey at times.
P ink and purple puddle jumper.
Y oung monster.

Erin Williford (6)
Goodrich CofE Primary School, Ross-On-Wye

Imogen

I ntelligent and kind.
M isty and cheerful.
O ne gloopy eye.
G iant and calm.
E ats lots.
N ice all the time.

Imogen Brewer (5)
Goodrich CofE Primary School, Ross-On-Wye

Tilly

T iny but strong
I nterested in maths
L oving and warm inside
L ikes to sing and dance
Y ellow eyes to make her happy.

Leilani Powell (7)
Goodrich CofE Primary School, Ross-On-Wye

Stripes

S miles
T ries different things
R ides a cow
I mmortal
P ositive
E xercises
S onic speed.

Benji Cowan (6)
Goodrich CofE Primary School, Ross-On-Wye

Bradly

B rave and intelligent
R oars like a lion
A trocious
D angerous to touch
L oves to play
Y oung age.

Flora Wimperis (6)
Goodrich CofE Primary School, Ross-On-Wye

Minnie

M innie and tiny
I ntelligent
N ever naughty
N ibbles on walls
I nvisible at night
E ggs he likes.

Daisy Ryan (6)
Goodrich CofE Primary School, Ross-On-Wye

Aliser

A loving monster
L icky monster
I cky monster
S illy monster
E xcellent monster
R eally sticky.

Ayda Jones (6)
Goodrich CofE Primary School, Ross-On-Wye

Sloppy

S lippery and angry
L ong and thin
O range and red
P erfect and wild
P uppy walker
Y ellow head.

Cai Malbon (7)
Goodrich CofE Primary School, Ross-On-Wye

Holly

H appy all the time
O bviously a genius
L oves to eat noodles
L oving hugs for everyone
Y ellow laser eyes.

Frankie Stretton (5)
Goodrich CofE Primary School, Ross-On-Wye

Edlie

E ldest monster,
D angerous and brave,
L oving friend,
I ncluding bad monsters,
E ye-tastic knowledge.

Elsie Neal (6)
Goodrich CofE Primary School, Ross-On-Wye

Giant

G ooey and slimy.
I nky with love.
A bsolutely friendly.
N asty spikes.
T rusting and intelligent.

Aster Summers (7)
Goodrich CofE Primary School, Ross-On-Wye

Timmy

T immy the monster.
I s responsible for people.
M isses out on food.
M ouldy fur.
Y ucky tongue.

Isaac Boyd (7)
Goodrich CofE Primary School, Ross-On-Wye

Bubble

B ig teeth
U nfriendly
B ig arms
B lack and green
L ots of arms
E vil chatter.

Ralph Radbone (7)
Goodrich CofE Primary School, Ross-On-Wye

Slobby

S lobby and gooey
L ives in a slimy cave
O riginal monster
B ad
B rave
Y oung.

Gracie Hallett (7)
Goodrich CofE Primary School, Ross-On-Wye

Spike

S wings on ropes
P roud back flipping
I cy around him
K ing of the monsters
E ats pizza.

Asa James (6)
Goodrich CofE Primary School, Ross-On-Wye

Sonic

S mall and lovely
O range long hair
N ice and blue
I ce cream and
C hicken he eats.

Albert Symonds (6)
Goodrich CofE Primary School, Ross-On-Wye

Flappy

F riendly
L oves to laugh
A nnoying
P opping bananas
P arty fun
Y oung.

William Brewer (6)
Goodrich CofE Primary School, Ross-On-Wye

Dotty

D otty the monster
O range fur
T alented monster
T ells the time
Y ellow eyes.

Eleanor Johnson (6)
Goodrich CofE Primary School, Ross-On-Wye

Betty

B ehaving well
E legant monster
T acky monster
T eething well
Y oung monster.

Alys Townsend (5)
Goodrich CofE Primary School, Ross-On-Wye

Salty

S oft fur
A mazing at climbing
L ots of spots
T errific fangs
Y ellow wings.

Merry Cox (6)
Goodrich CofE Primary School, Ross-On-Wye

Sliby

S limy and slim
L oving and liked
I ntelligent
B lack eyes
Y ellow fur.

Gabriel Beattie (7)
Goodrich CofE Primary School, Ross-On-Wye

Boby

B lue and purple
O range hair
B lack is his favourite colour
Y oung monster.

Andie Emblen (6)
Goodrich CofE Primary School, Ross-On-Wye

Asid

A ngry and black
S mart but mean
I nteresting monster
D isgusting and wild.

Sammy Van Marsh (6)
Goodrich CofE Primary School, Ross-On-Wye

Rose

R ed and pink
O ne monster
S miles happily
E veryone's favourite.

Athena Jones-Davies (5)
Goodrich CofE Primary School, Ross-On-Wye

Jorg

J olly Jorg
O ctopus monster
R ed and white
G iant tentacles.

Freddy Byrne (7)
Goodrich CofE Primary School, Ross-On-Wye

Koopa Troopas

K nows how to be bad
O verly angry
O verly mean
P owerful
A ttacks

T errible
R ude
O verly powerful
O verly tactical
P inches
A wful
S uper surprising.

Jack Moore (7)
Hall Orchard CE Primary School, Barrow upon Soar

Mr Horrace

M y friend
R eally likes me

H e plays with me
O f course I like him too
R acing each other
R unning around
A nd having lots of fun
C aring, sharing
E veryone join the fun.

Charlie Padgett (5)
Hall Orchard CE Primary School, Barrow upon Soar

Blobby

B lobby, turn around
L ook at me and touch the ground
O ff you go, get a cookie
B ehind is the park, don't get mucky
B lobby, Blobby, you are so kind
Y ou're my best friend, you're always on my mind.

Evie Caren (5)
Hall Orchard CE Primary School, Barrow upon Soar

Meatball

M eatball monster is made of meatballs
E xcellent spaghetti hair
A ble to walk
T eaches tricks
B ananas are his favourite
A nd ants
L oud laugh
L ots of fun.

Isaac Kalsi (5)
Hall Orchard CE Primary School, Barrow upon Soar

Scruffy

S cruffy is smelly
C ries when he gets wet
R uns and hides when it rains
U mbrellas help him best
F unny and loud
F luffy and furry
Y our favourite monster, Scruffy.

Harlow Bowler (6)
Hall Orchard CE Primary School, Barrow upon Soar

Bubbles

B ubbles likes to play with bubbles,
U p in the air,
B ouncing high and low,
B ack and forth,
L oves making friends,
E ating stones,
S tops her floating away.

Martha Graham-Hind (5)
Hall Orchard CE Primary School, Barrow upon Soar

Grumpy

G rumpy is what I call my monster
R ound head and a big eye
U nder a bush is where he hides
M y worst monster
P urple is his colour
Y ou would not like my monster.

Emilia S (6)
Hall Orchard CE Primary School, Barrow upon Soar

Switch

S witch the monster
W inged hands for flying
I ncredible at football
T hinks toes are interesting
C olourful and bright
H e is hilarious at telling jokes.

Miller Walton (6)
Hall Orchard CE Primary School, Barrow upon Soar

Master Hawk Eye

H awk Eye is my name.
A lion monster.
W ings that are invisible.
K ings of monsters.

E yes like lasers.
Y ellow chest.
E ats slime.

Oliver Nutting (6)
Hall Orchard CE Primary School, Barrow upon Soar

Purple

P urple is a spider monster,
U nder the bed he hides,
R uns and catches flies,
P uts them in his web,
L ikes eating flies with slime,
E yes are green!

Harry Moulds (6)
Hall Orchard CE Primary School, Barrow upon Soar

Blue Fur

B ook lover
L oves to play
U nder chairs
E ats the crumbs

F allen on the floor
U rgh! He eats fluff too
R ugs are his favourite.

Violet Laywood (6)
Hall Orchard CE Primary School, Barrow upon Soar

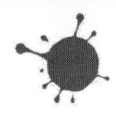

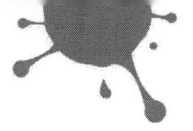

Scruffy The Monster

S he is smelly
C hatty, cheeky monster
R eads lots of books
U nique
F unny
F luffy
Y ells really loud, that's Scruffy the monster.

Sophia Penn (5)
Hall Orchard CE Primary School, Barrow upon Soar

Crunchy

C razy
R oly-poly
U nusual
N obody knows him
C an anybody see him? No
H ide if you see him
Y ou never know what he will do next.

Sophie Jasper (5)
Hall Orchard CE Primary School, Barrow upon Soar

Rosie

R osie is extremely funny.
O f course, she is friendly.
S he would like to be friends.
I would like to play with her.
E very day, she comes to play.

Eloise Riley (7)
Hall Orchard CE Primary School, Barrow upon Soar

Spikey

S pikey is really angry.
P ink arm is what Spikey has.
I have spikes all over my body.
K riss kross eyes.
E ars are small.
Y ellow legs.

Huey Woodrup (7)
Hall Orchard CE Primary School, Barrow upon Soar

Crunchie

C razy monster Crunchie
R uns fast
U nbeatable
N aughty boy
C ute
H e is strong
I s happy
E ats lots of broccoli.

Arthur Goddard (6)
Hall Orchard CE Primary School, Barrow upon Soar

Rainbow

R eally long legs
A rms wiggle
I t only eats plants
N ails like razors
B ig sharp teeth
O range eyes
W onderful colours.

Forest Stewart (6)
Hall Orchard CE Primary School, Barrow upon Soar

Stormy

S tomp, stomp all the way
T rying to be mean
O h! I wonder why
R eally? Yes, really
M ean? Yes, mean
Y ikes! What a scary monster.

Heidi Jewitt (6)
Hall Orchard CE Primary School, Barrow upon Soar

Greedy George

G runts when he's hungry.
E ats lots of jelly.
O nly has eight eyes.
R eally furry.
G ood at ball games.
E verybody loves him.

Abel Sharpe (6)
Hall Orchard CE Primary School, Barrow upon Soar

Floppy

F loppy the monster
L oves to eat bugs
O nly likes playing
P arts of him are pink
P layday is his favourite thing
Y ells a lot.

Frankie Ross (6)
Hall Orchard CE Primary School, Barrow upon Soar

Nibbles

N ose is black
I s orange
B ig, bright eyes
B eautiful
L ovely dancing
E ats naughty grown-ups
S hiny, fluffy hair.

Eden Turner (5)
Hall Orchard CE Primary School, Barrow upon Soar

Sophia

S ophia is kind
O lives are her favourite
P lays music loudly
H as soft rainbow fur
I s incredibly funny
A nd is always happy!

Mia Seaton (5)
Hall Orchard CE Primary School, Barrow upon Soar

Slimy

S limy the monster
L oves to eat lemons
I think he's cheeky
M y friends think he's fluffy
Y ou may think he's colourful.

Morgan Hitchcock (5)
Hall Orchard CE Primary School, Barrow upon Soar

Octo's Song

O cto's tentacles wiggle and wave
C ape is gold, shiny, he's so brave
T en creepy eyes glow so bright
O cto keeps us safe every night.

Elijah Nagra (5)
Hall Orchard CE Primary School, Barrow upon Soar

The Spooky Monster

- **S** pooky monster is slimy
- **P** oos a lot
- **O** ne oval-shaped eye
- **O** range, hairy skin
- **K** angaroos are his friend
- **Y** ellow sick!

Daisy Vickers (5)
Hall Orchard CE Primary School, Barrow upon Soar

Squiggly

- **S** tinky
- **Q** uiet
- **U** bby is his friend
- **I** gloo house
- **G** iggly
- **G** oogly eyes
- **L** oves sleep
- **Y** oung.

Owen Clithero (5)
Hall Orchard CE Primary School, Barrow upon Soar

Electric

- **E** nergetic
- **L** ovely
- **E** ats healthy
- **C** alm
- **T** ries hard
- **R** uns fast
- **I** ntelligent
- **C** uddles Leo.

Leo Hopkinson (5)
Hall Orchard CE Primary School, Barrow upon Soar

Jeffrey

J umps up and down
E ats snakes
F unny
F riendly
R uns fast
E xcellent at everything
Y awns a lot.

Teddy Barkby (6)
Hall Orchard CE Primary School, Barrow upon Soar

My Mr Happy

M akes me smile
R ugby player.

H appy
A mazing
P ointy horns
P ointy toes
Y oghurt eater.

Arthur Evans (6)
Hall Orchard CE Primary School, Barrow upon Soar

Grummy

G rummy is grumpy
R ed skin
U nhappy always
M ardy and mumbly
M umbly and mardy
Y ou stay away from Grummy!

Isobella Morris (7)
Hall Orchard CE Primary School, Barrow upon Soar

The Slimy Monster

S he is a scary girl
L ikes eating slime
I like scaring people
M y body is very slimy
Y ellow is my favourite colour.

Anaiya Arefin (6)
Hall Orchard CE Primary School, Barrow upon Soar

Bloo Is Furry

B loo, the furry monster.
L oves sausages with potatoes.
O ver the rainbow is where he lives.
O ne big blue eye to see you with.

Archie Savage (5)
Hall Orchard CE Primary School, Barrow upon Soar

Reuben

- **R** uns everywhere
- **E** ats everything
- **U** nusual smell
- **B** ad hair
- **E** njoys playing football
- **N** othing can stop me.

Reuben Landon (5)
Hall Orchard CE Primary School, Barrow upon Soar

Giggles

G roovy
I mportant
G assy
G iggly
L aughs a lot
E ggy trumps
S tinky, smelly and smiley.

Emily Williams (6)
Hall Orchard CE Primary School, Barrow upon Soar

Gloopy

G loopy the superhero
L ong legs
O range eyes
O tto is his friend
P atchy skin
Y ou will be scared.

Louis Young (5)
Hall Orchard CE Primary School, Barrow upon Soar

My Best Friend

S limy, slippery monster
I love him
L oves lemony lemonade
L ittle bit loopy
Y ou are my yellow best friend.

Ellie Marston (5)
Hall Orchard CE Primary School, Barrow upon Soar

Kongzi

K icks monsters
O pens big mouth
N oisy roar
G rey body
Z igzag pointy spine
I t lives in caves.

Hussein Abbas (6)
Hall Orchard CE Primary School, Barrow upon Soar

Jelly Monster

J ust a jelly blob
E ating pink slime
L oving the taste
L ook at his arms
Y ou wouldn't believe it.

George Squires (6)
Hall Orchard CE Primary School, Barrow upon Soar

Swirly

S limy
W eird
I t smells bad
R ubbish at handwriting
L ong, sharp claws
Y ellow monster.

Lily Broderick (7)
Hall Orchard CE Primary School, Barrow upon Soar

Spooks

S uper fury
P ointy horns
O rangey-red eyes
O dd green fur
K iller fangs
S cary claws.

George Hickling (6)
Hall Orchard CE Primary School, Barrow upon Soar

Vivi

V ivi is happy
I ron is what Vivi is made of
V est is what Vivi wears
I ce cream is what Vivi likes to eat.

Halle Woodrup (5)
Hall Orchard CE Primary School, Barrow upon Soar

Flops

F lops is a monster
L ow to the floor is he
O dd-shaped body
P astel purple
S ee him and run.

Francesca R (6)
Hall Orchard CE Primary School, Barrow upon Soar

Slime

S lime the monster
L ives in Slime Land
I s friendly
M akes a yucky smell
E ats slimy food.

Jack Perkins (5)
Hall Orchard CE Primary School, Barrow upon Soar

Furry

F urry is his name
U nder the bed
R eady to cuddle
R elaxing and nice
Y ay, he's great!

Adelaide Quinn (6)
Hall Orchard CE Primary School, Barrow upon Soar

Redy The Monster

R edy is happy.
E very day she eats fish.
D own by the sea, she lives in a cave.
Y ou know she is red?

Bethan Noble (5)
Hall Orchard CE Primary School, Barrow upon Soar

My Monster Monster

R oars out slime
A pples and worms he loves
R ides a rocket to the moon
A lways looking for adventure.

James Slade (6)
Hall Orchard CE Primary School, Barrow upon Soar

Slobby

S limy
L ikes goo
O range tongue
B ow tie
B lue body
Y oga is his favourite.

Piper Winfield (5)
Hall Orchard CE Primary School, Barrow upon Soar

Slimy

S limy is silly
L ives in a cave
I ts fur is green
M akes a lot of noise
Y ellow teeth.

Jackson Turner (6)
Hall Orchard CE Primary School, Barrow upon Soar

Spiky

S piky the monster
P lays with everyone
I tches himself
K icks footballs
Y ellow face.

Maryam Abbas (5)
Hall Orchard CE Primary School, Barrow upon Soar

Pinky

P ink fur
I ncredible spikes
N ine yellow eyes
K ind and bouncy
Y our pink fun friend.

Freya Adams (5)
Hall Orchard CE Primary School, Barrow upon Soar

Clawy

C reepy monster
L oves to eat children
A lways out at night
W erewolf
Y ellow teeth.

Maxwell Smith (5)
Hall Orchard CE Primary School, Barrow upon Soar

Theo

T heo the monster
H e shouts everywhere
E lectric doesn't work on him
O ne sharp tooth.

Theo Dunn (5)
Hall Orchard CE Primary School, Barrow upon Soar

Pull

P ull is kind
U ltimate chocolate eater
L oves to lie down
L egs are green with springy feet.

Willow Pymm (5)
Hall Orchard CE Primary School, Barrow upon Soar

Hairy

H ungry belly
A wesome teeth
I ts tongue is green
R ed eyes
Y ellow ears.

Max Copeman (5)
Hall Orchard CE Primary School, Barrow upon Soar

Bloat

B ig body
L ittle legs
O range fur
A lways happy
T otally awesome.

Cassandra Crawshaw (5)
Hall Orchard CE Primary School, Barrow upon Soar

Grummy

G reedy
R ude
U nbelievably
M ean
M ad
Y oyo.

William Morris (6)
Hall Orchard CE Primary School, Barrow upon Soar

Fred

F red the monster
R eads a book
E ven likes to run
D irty knees.

Jago Cohill IV (6)
Hall Orchard CE Primary School, Barrow upon Soar

My Monster Furry

F un
U tterly fun
R ed
R eally red
Y ummy slime.

Lydia Andrews (6)
Hall Orchard CE Primary School, Barrow upon Soar

Boo

B oo is the monster
O ne big spike
O nly red on his body.

Neve Morris (5)
Hall Orchard CE Primary School, Barrow upon Soar

Tig

T ig loves running
I ckle red eyes
G rey spiky hair.

Ivy Hamilton (5)
Hall Orchard CE Primary School, Barrow upon Soar

Peeps

P eeps is a respectful monster
E very day for breakfast he eats yummy pancakes
E very day he goes swimming and goes to football club
P eeps has lots of fun
S o the next day he goes to soft play.

Perla Shehaj (6)
Hurst Park Primary School, West Molesey

Fluffy

F luffy likes to play tennis.
L oves learning every day.
U sually eats an apple every day.
F luffy, purple eyes.
F luffy's favourite food is chocolate cake.
Y ellow, long fur.

Isabelle Levitt (7)
Hurst Park Primary School, West Molesey

Crazy Bob

C hocolate birthday cake is his favourite
R iding horses
A small minion
Z any
Y ellow.

B right
O range saddle
B lack feet.

Lily Clarke (6)
Hurst Park Primary School, West Molesey

Bloby

B loby is a kind friend.
L oves playing with his friends.
O h no, he spilt his Cherry Coke!
B ig mind every day.
Y ou are lucky if you see Bloby.

Jack N (7)
Hurst Park Primary School, West Molesey

Slime

S lime eats slime for dinner,
L ittle time to eat slime,
I nside the mud is slime,
M oney in Slime's hand,
E xcitingly Slime is slimy!

Miri (6)
Hurst Park Primary School, West Molesey

Rose

R ose likes to go to school and play.
O ne pink, googly eye.
S ometimes Rose has really good behaviour.
E ats healthy food like apples, and bananas.

Ruby Pemberton (6)
Hurst Park Primary School, West Molesey

Holly

H elpful Holly is kind and unique
O ffering to help her adults
L oving and creating
L oves to make new friends
Y oyoing about sharing.

Emily Jacklin (7)
Hurst Park Primary School, West Molesey

Andy

A kind, thoughtful monster
N o fruit and vegetables he loves
D oes he like dinosaurs?
Y es, he does like dinosaurs, just the right amount.

Akira De Rijk (6)
Hurst Park Primary School, West Molesey

Furry

F antastic behaviour
U ni is great for her
R espectful all the time
R osy cheeks
Y ou better watch out because Furry is about.

Alba Wragg (6)
Hurst Park Primary School, West Molesey

Blogzy

B ob eats every day
L ikes dogs
O ver the years he ate
G oing on holiday
Z ebras in his house
Y ummy cake.

Adam Nowogrodzki (7)
Hurst Park Primary School, West Molesey

Lola

L ola gets dirty.
O live and Lola together.
L oves to play with friends.
A ll of the Lolas are kind.

Ryan Rouine (6)
Hurst Park Primary School, West Molesey

Pecy

P eaceful and calm
E xcited
C hewy mouth
Y ou love looking at her when she talks.

Chloe Chapman (6)
Hurst Park Primary School, West Molesey

Ghosty

G rotty
H orrifying
O nly in the deep, dark woods
S cary bubbles
T oxic juice
Y ucky monster.

Stephanie McGonigle (7)
Mossvale Primary School, Paisley

Slimy Monster

S potty as a dog
L ime green
I n Mars
M onster is large
Y ucky monster.

Raaeid Jumahi Ahmed (7)
Mossvale Primary School, Paisley

Cute

C urious cloud
U p in the night sky
T iny sparkles
E xciting monster.

Harper Logan (7)
Mossvale Primary School, Paisley

Ghost

G host the invisible
H orrid
O minous
S cary
T errifying.

Callen Fairbairn
Mossvale Primary School, Paisley

Cute

C uriously sweet
U nique
T iny as a mouse
E xcitingly fun.

Beth Beaton (7)
Mossvale Primary School, Paisley

Sharp Claw The Monster

S neaky movements
H owling in the wind
A wfully big claws
R oaring in the distance
P rowling quietly

C laws that stretch
L urking in the dark
A ncient creature
W ailing in the wind.

Molly Colquhoun (6)
Muirhouse Primary School, Motherwell

Monster Boo The Monster

M assive footprints
O ozing with goo
N asty fangs
S piky tail
T owering tall
E vil grin
R oaring in the trees.

B ig and bold
O ddly shaped
O verwhelmingly big.

Alex Neary (6)
Muirhouse Primary School, Motherwell

Furliy Boo The Monster

F lying powers
U nstoppable
R oaring noises
L urking in the dark
I nvisible in the dark
Y owling sounds.

B ouncing body
O ozing with goo
O utstanding body.

Latifa Abasi (6)
Muirhouse Primary School, Motherwell

Choo Choo The Monster

C racking bones
H owling wind
O ozing with goo
O ddly shaped

C racking bones
H owling wind
O ozing with goo
O ddly shaped.

Reggie Buchan (6)
Muirhouse Primary School, Motherwell

Bobbles The Monster

B ig and bold
O ozing with goo
B ellowing loudly
B ouncing blob
L urking in the dark
E vil grin
S limy skin.

Reegan Macdonald (6)
Muirhouse Primary School, Motherwell

Harleigh The Monster

H ungry
A ngry
R attling breath
L ong sharp teeth
E motional
I cy stare
G lowing eyes
H airy.

Ariannah O'Connor (6)
Muirhouse Primary School, Motherwell

Monster Acrostics - Poetic Charms

Googles The Monster

G lowing eyes
O ozing with goo
O ddly shaped
G lowing noises
L umpy and bumpy
E vil grin
S piky tail.

Logan Rattray (7)
Muirhouse Primary School, Motherwell

Ela Boo The Monster

E erie glow
L urking in the dark
A ngry roars.

B eautiful
O ozing with goo
O ddly shaped.

Skyla McLean (8)
Muirhouse Primary School, Motherwell

Smiley The Monster

S piky tail
M assive footprints
I cy stare
L ong sharp claws
E normous feet
Y awning loudly.

Holly Montgomery (7)
Muirhouse Primary School, Motherwell

Sparky The Monster

S trong
P erfect
A ngry
R ight foot creep
K iller
Y ellow fangs.

Oliver Steele (7)
Muirhouse Primary School, Motherwell

Spike The Monster

S piky tail
P ointy ears
I cy stare
K ing of the night
E erie glow.

Amelia McCulloch (6)
Muirhouse Primary School, Motherwell

Jack The Monster

J umping through shadows
A wesome grin
C racking bones
K ing of the night.

Louie Stewart (7)
Muirhouse Primary School, Motherwell

Fang The Monster

F unny and fearless
A ngry
N oisy
G rowly.

Bella Richardson (6)
Muirhouse Primary School, Motherwell

Boom The Monster

B est monster
O n task
O ozing
M assive.

Ezra Baxter (7)
Muirhouse Primary School, Motherwell

Slimy The Slime Monster

S limy the slime monster,
A s green as a green highlighter.
T he red bones of him are so cool
U nder the sun as they shine purple.
R un away, you might think, but he's friendly.
D o feel free to touch him as he'll be friends,
A nd in his diet are big cats, like cheetahs,
Y ou can also give him food if he's at a park.

Arjun Singh Rathore (7)
Park Lane Primary School, Wembley

Fluffys

F luffys is her name and having fun is her game.
L ots of eyes to see far and wide.
U nderground she likes to hide.
F lowers are her favourite food.
F erocious roars she makes when she is in a bad mood.
Y ou should come to the forest before the day ends.
S oon enough you'll be the best of friends.

Allanah Trinidad (6)
Park Lane Primary School, Wembley

Munchball

M unchball has a big mouth
U nfriendly to his friend, and mean
N one of his friends lie
C runching, dirty feet
H ungry eyes and mouth like he's hungry
B all eyes like a football
A happy smile on his face
L oves to eat candy sweets
L ies to other monsters.

Myra Patel (6)
Park Lane Primary School, Wembley

Twinkle: A Shiny Monster

T winkly wings that shine bright.
W andering in the forest where stars are aligned.
I n the dark, magic is near.
N ighttime friend who brings good cheer.
K ind and soft, it keeps everyone warm.
L ittle sparkling with a very big charm.
E very heart wants this gem.

Arhaan Momin (7)
Park Lane Primary School, Wembley

Alien Burn The Monster

A lways makes people angry and is never helpful
L ikes to snatch treats
I t sprints quickly
E ats mice
N aughty as a thief

B ig and bouncy belly
U ses his eyes like antennae
R ed shiny ears
N ose is just a hole.

Jacob Rai (6)
Park Lane Primary School, Wembley

Mighty

M agnificent monster, with scales of green
I ncredibly strong, the strongest ever seen
G rinning wide, with teeth so sharp and long
H uge and hairy, where he does belong
T errifying roars, echoing through the land
Y ummy snacks, a juicy, plump hand.

Amay Gupta (6)
Park Lane Primary School, Wembley

The Dangerous Monster

D otty monster
A ngry when hungry
N aughty and shouty
G reen, ghosty body
E ats humans
R uns faster
O ne googly eye
U nder the bed
S cary, makes someone worry.

Nitya Patel (7)
Park Lane Primary School, Wembley

Spikes

S hadow moves through the trees
P ointy spikes sway in the breeze
I n the dark, I make no sound
K eeping quiet on the ground
E veryone runs when I appear
S caring them, I disappear.

Priyansh Solanki (7)
Park Lane Primary School, Wembley

Shrink

S hrink is scary
H e's fuzzy and purple and blue
R eally smelly and doesn't wash at all
I s tough and strong
N eeds to eat fruit and vegetables
K eeps treasure in a vault.

Kiriana Bellingy (7)
Park Lane Primary School, Wembley

Rainbow

R ainbow is my name
A lways I am angry
I have four sharp horns
N osy
B ounces everywhere
O range eyes, I have ten
W obbly jelly is what I love to eat.

Kyle Allen (7)
Park Lane Primary School, Wembley

Slumfy

S mall little monster
L oves to jump in the dumpster
U nless it is sunset - this
M onster won't be outside
F urry, scary and lumpy
Y et I named her Slumfy.

Miruzaini Ravichandran (7)
Park Lane Primary School, Wembley

Taboy

T all and watching in the night
A ll the kids are filled with fright
B ig and furry with eyes so dark
O n the run, ready to bite
Y ells and shouts, run from sight.

Ilyas Nouar (6)
Park Lane Primary School, Wembley

Spooky, Scary Bobby

B ooing is disliked by Bobby,
O pen-minded and also positive,
B oisterous and has a lot of energy,
B ig, googly eyes,
Y earning to not get in trouble.

Aiden D'Silva (7)
Park Lane Primary School, Wembley

Mikey

M ikey likes Maltesers
I ce cream is his favourite
K ellogg's he has for breakfast
E ye - he has one
Y oung and full of life.

Ayaan Hanif (7)
Park Lane Primary School, Wembley

Bumpy

B umpy the monster
U gly but friendly
M akes slimy cakes
P repares scary parties
Y ummy! Yucky! That's my friend.

Emma Taraba Donati (7)
Park Lane Primary School, Wembley

Silly

S tinky little monster
I nteresting bubbles around his head
L oves to be messy and
L urks beneath...
Y our bed.

Anha Jadav (8)
Park Lane Primary School, Wembley

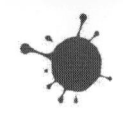

My Silly Acrostic

S o silly
T oo funny jokes
I cy, sticky fur
C ool spots and claws
K ind attitude
Y ucky, slimy fur.

Nylah Jackson (7)
Park Lane Primary School, Wembley

Sovak The Monster

S ovak is slimy
O range coloured
V egetarian
A rmless monster
K ind monster.

Mayra Patil (6)
Park Lane Primary School, Wembley

Shiny

S plendid hair
H igh spirited
I ce blue teeth
N ice eye
Y ellow face.

Anna Bacso (7)
Park Lane Primary School, Wembley

Blod's Friend

B lod loves slimes
L oves to play with slime
O utside, inside all the time
D ance together in the weather
S lime loves Blod

F riends forever and together
R ight in their home
I nside, they're outside now, always playing
E ric also joins in painting
N ever do Blod and their friends fall out
D o you think they ever shout?

Eric Botwright (7)
Romanby Primary School, Romanby

Bird Monster

B ird monster likes to fly
I t lives in a tree up high
R adishes are its favourite food
D idn't he get in a mood?

M etal is its worst material
O ne little bird
N attering in its nest
S itting in its tree
T eeth like rocks
E normous jaws
R eady to eat you.

George Hartley (7)
Romanby Primary School, Romanby

Slimer

S limer fighting with his friend Blob.
L oves his friend Blob.
I like chasing Slimer and Blob.
M oves swiftly and smoothly.
E ats mouldy, sweaty socks.
R ound spots on his belly.

Layla Grant (7)
Romanby Primary School, Romanby

My Marvellous Pet Monster

M arvellous monster munches Monster Munch
R eads ridiculous rhymes

F antastic Fox has lots of fun
O ut and about having fun with friends
X -ray vision eyes at night.

Archie Miles (7)
Romanby Primary School, Romanby

Cyclops

C ircular nose
Y ellow dirty teeth
C urly tail
L ikes to scare
O ne scary eye
P ink sharp horns
S caly green skin.

Joshua Morris (7)
Romanby Primary School, Romanby

Slimy

S uper slimy
L ovely and rhymey
I think he's at my door
M y floor is slippery
"Y ou will clean this up, Slimy!"

Evie Parkes (7)
Romanby Primary School, Romanby

Roblox

R oblox the monster
O ne googly eye
B rown, sharp teeth
L oves to hide
O range is his colour
X -ray vision.

Matthew Paul (6)
Romanby Primary School, Romanby

Sakul The Monster

S o serious
A lways hungry
K ing of the monsters
U ltimate strength
L oves his family.

Lukas Bishop (6)
Romanby Primary School, Romanby

Snog

S nuggly Snog
N ice
O pen-hearted
G inormous.

Thomas Field (6)
Romanby Primary School, Romanby

My Monster Is Called Sprinkles

S prinkles is a very happy monster
P lays outside in Monsterland
R eally fluffy fur that is blue
I s shorter than all of the other monsters
N ever enough sprinkles
K eeps a secret stash of sprinkles in his ears
L oves rainbow sprinkles
E ats sprinkles for breakfast, lunch and dinner
S prinkles is a special monster.

Lucilla Gargaro (8)
St Dominic's Primary School, Airdrie

Bubbles

B lue, funny monster.
U nderstands how to stay healthy.
B ubbles is a smelly monster.
B ubbles is a furry monster.
L oves to play games.
E ats apples all day.
S melly hair that looks like snakes.

Cierra Lafferty (7)
St Dominic's Primary School, Airdrie

Orangey

- **O** range fur
- **R** ed details on his horns
- **A** bsolutely adorable
- **N** ice personality
- **G** ets into the cabinets and steals oranges
- **E** nergy is really high
- **Y** ellow horns with red strokes.

Maya Szydlowska (7)
St Dominic's Primary School, Airdrie

Noodles

N oodles is long and stringy
O range oozy skin
O bstacles are good to win
D oodles around
L ikes to sing rock music
E ats ice cream
S ells slime to his monster friends.

Willow Drummond (7)
St Dominic's Primary School, Airdrie

Sharpy

S harp teeth, sharp claws, big claws on feet and sharp ears
H appy monster that always smiles
A round purple body
R ed big eyes
P urple fur
Y ellow spiky bits of fur.

Sara Marczak (7)
St Dominic's Primary School, Airdrie

Swarly

S warly likes wind, it
W hirls all over him.
A lways friendly.
R eally likes to eat slime.
L ikes everyone in the world.
Y ellow fur on the sides.

Anthony Adeoye (7)
St Dominic's Primary School, Airdrie

Crazy

C ute little face like a baby
R eally curly red hair
A lways sad
Z ebras are her favourite animal
Y ellow ice cream is all she eats.

Katie N McAspurren (8)
St Dominic's Primary School, Airdrie

Dubby

D oesn't like animals
U nderstands other languages
B ig scary claws
B ig ears for hearing
Y ellow glow in the dark toenails.

Reuben Graham (7)
St Dominic's Primary School, Airdrie

Bows

B ows really loves wearing bows.
O wns 1000 bows.
W onderful pink fluffy fur.
S uper happy monster all the time.

Charlotte Watson (7)
St Dominic's Primary School, Airdrie

Tricks

T all monster
R ainbow monster
I s scary
C an do tricks
K ind to everyone
S o nice.

Anton Hamill (7)
St Dominic's Primary School, Airdrie

Soft Paws

S oft Paws is a princess and a doctor
O ne best friend called Cini
F amily time is her favourite
T reats people when they are poorly

P ink (hot) is her colour
A lways eats chicken skin, cherries and ice cream
W hen she falls, she lands on her feet
S tops children from saying mean words.

Aveline Gazzani (5)
St George's School, Edgbaston

All About Monsters

M any creatures, big and small
O ut in the woods, they crouch and crawl
N ever scary, just fun and friendly
S ome are slimy, some are hairy
T hey are playful and funny
E verywhere they run and hide
R eally, monsters are just happy and kind.

Abaan Shams (5)
St George's School, Edgbaston

Harpy

H arpy is a happy monster
A pples are his favourite fruit
R unning is his favourite sport
P eas are his favourite vegetable
Y ellow is the colour of his fur.

Ajai Choudhary (7)
St George's School, Edgbaston

Slimey

S cary monster
L ikes to slither
I n my bedroom
M ommy is scared
E veryone is frightened
Y ou do not have to be scared.

Abigail Tonks (6)
St George's School, Edgbaston

Fluffy

F urry and small
L ikes to crawl
U nder the bed
F eeding on dread
F riendly disguise
Y et full of surprise.

Sabina Tomenchuk (6)
St George's School, Edgbaston

Daisy

D aisy is my pet.
A wesome tiny monster.
I love her.
S he is beautiful.
Y ellow, pink, red, grey, blue and black.

Amelia Boutefnouchet (5)
St George's School, Edgbaston

Chummy

C hummy is my pet
H e is a treasure
U nbelievable
M y best chum
M ighty cheerful
Y ellow skin.

Zayan Nasar (6)
St George's School, Edgbaston

Bobby

B obby is a good friend
O ne wobbly eye
B obby is silly
B obby likes to eat cake
Y ummy yummy!

Danyil Mamus (6)
St George's School, Edgbaston

Sammy

S ammy likes to wiggle
A nd he is enormous
M unches on muffins
M mmm
Y ummy yummy!

Arya Adil (5)
St George's School, Edgbaston

Young Writers Information

We hope you have enjoyed reading this book – and that you will continue to in the coming years.

If you're the parent or family member of an enthusiastic poet or story writer, do visit our website **www.youngwriters.co.uk/subscribe** and sign up to receive news, competitions, writing challenges and tips, activities and much, much more! There's lots to keep budding writers motivated!

If you would like to order further copies of this book, or any of our other titles, then please give us a call or order via your online account.

Young Writers
Remus House
Coltsfoot Drive
Peterborough
PE2 9BF
(01733) 890066
info@youngwriters.co.uk

**Join in the conversation!
Tips, news, giveaways and much more!**

YoungWritersUK   YoungWritersCW
youngwriterscw   youngwriterscw

Scan Me!